FROM **FARM** TO FOOD

Where Does Fruit Come From?

Linda Staniford

capstone

To contact Capstone Global Library please call 800-747-4992,
or visit our web site www.capstonepub.com

Edited by Helen Cox Cannons
Designed by Steve Mead
Original illustrations © Capstone Global Library Limited 2016
Illustrated by Steve Mead
Picture research by Tracy Cummins
Production by Victoria Fitzgerald
Originated by Capstone Global Library Limited

Library of Congress Cataloging-in-Publication Data
Names: Staniford, Linda, author. | Staniford, Linda. From farm
to fork.
Title: Where does fruit come from? / by Linda Staniford.
Other titles: Heinemann read and learn.
Description: Chicago, Illinois : Heinemann-Raintree, [2016] |
Series: From
 farm to fork | Series: Heinemann read and learn | Includes
bibliographical
 references and index.
Identifiers: LCCN 2015043860|
 ISBN 9781484633526 (library binding)
 ISBN 9781484633564 (paperback)
 ISBN 9781484633601 (ebook pdf)
Subjects: LCSH: Oranges--Juvenile literature. | Fruit--Juvenile
literature.
Classification: LCC SB370.O7 S83 2016 | DDC 634--dc23

Acknowledgments
The author and publisher are grateful to the following for
permission to reproduce copyright material: Alamy: foto-
mix, 16, Marwood jenkins, 18; Corbis: Momatiuk - Eastcott,
9, Paulo Fridman, 15; Getty Images: Camille Tokerud, 21,
ROBERT SULLIVAN/AFP, 12; iStockphoto: GeorgeDolgikh,
17; Newscom: Michele Molinari/DanitaDelimont.com, 14;
Shutterstock: Africa Studio, Cover Right, 5, Alex Staroseltsev,
23 Bottom Middle, Alf Ribeiro, 8, apiguide, Cover Left,
Deymos.HR, 11, EvrenKalinbacak, 19, images72, 6, Jim Parkin,
Cover Back, 10, Maks Narodenko, 23 Top, 23 Top Middle, 23
Middle, Marco Ossino, 13, MO_SES Premium, 4, Tim UR, 23
Bottom, vladimir salman, 7, Voronin76, 20.

Every effort has been made to contact copyright holders
of material reproduced in this book. Any omissions will
be rectified in subsequent printings if notice is given to
the publisher.

Some words are shown in bold, **like this**. You can find out
what they mean by looking in the glossary.

Table of Contents

What Are Fruits?

Fruits come from plants. Fruits can grow on bushes or trees. The fruit is the part of the plant that contains seeds. Seeds make new plants.

Fruits are an important part of our diet.
The fruits we eat give us **vitamins**.
Vitamins keep our bodies healthy.

Where Do Fruits Grow?

Fruits grow all over the world. Fruits can be grown on large or small farms. Some fruits grow in **orchards**.

You can even grow some kinds of fruit yourself. In this book we will look at how oranges get from farms to your plate.

How Are Oranges Planted?

Oranges grow on trees. The trees start their life as seeds. The seeds are planted in pots. Orange trees then grow from these seeds.

When the orange trees have grown big enough, they are planted in an **orchard**. It can take around five years before they have oranges growing on them.

How Do Oranges Grow?

In the spring, orange trees grow flowers called **blossoms**. The blossoms smell sweet and attract insects.

The blossoms die and fall off the trees.
Fruits grow instead. The fruits are small
and green at first, but get bigger and
turn orange as they **ripen**.

How Are Oranges Harvested?

When the oranges are **ripe**, they are **harvested**. Harvesting means picking a crop. Sometimes a machine is used to shake the trees. This makes the oranges fall off into a big tray.

Most oranges are harvested by hand. Harvesters climb ladders, pick the oranges, and put them into bags or crates.

What Happens After Harvesting?

After they have been **harvested**, the oranges are sorted by machine. Any oranges that are not suitable for eating are taken out. Then the oranges are washed.

Some oranges are used to make fruit juice. These oranges are taken to factories. There, the oranges are peeled and squeezed to get the juice out.

How Are Oranges Preserved?

Preserving is treating the fruit to stop it from going bad. Marmalade is a kind of preserve. It is like jam, but made from oranges.

The peel of the orange is used as well as the insides. The peel makes marmalade taste bitter. Sugar is added to sweeten it. Some types of oranges can also be preserved in cans.

What Happens to Oranges After Washing?

The oranges are packed in boxes and loaded onto trucks. The trucks take some of the oranges to stores and markets.

Others are taken to ports where they are loaded onto **cargo** ships. The ships take the oranges all over the world. They go to countries where oranges cannot grow.

How Do the Oranges Get to Our Table?

Workers put the oranges out on shelves in the stores. The oranges are ready for us to eat. There are a lot of other fruits in the stores as well.

When we go grocery shopping, we choose our oranges. The oranges have had a long journey from farm to fork!

All Kinds of Fruits!

There are many kinds of fruits. Some fruits only grow in hot countries. For example, mangoes grow in India and bananas grow in the Caribbean. Other fruits, such as apples and pears, grow in cooler places.

You can eat the seeds of some fruits, but not pits. Peaches have pits inside and we do not eat them. Strawberries have seeds on the outside. We eat them.

Glossary

blossom flower on a bush or tree

cargo objects carried by a ship, aircraft, or other vehicle

harvest pick a crop

orchard field or farm where fruit trees are grown

preserve keep something fresh. Fruits that have been made into jam or marmalade are called preserves.

ripe ready to pick and eat

vitamins good things in foods that help our bodies stay healthy

Find Out More

Books

Dickmann, Nancy. *Food from Farms* (World of Farming).
  Chicago: Heinemann Library, 2011.
Rooney, Anne. *Apples Grow on Trees* (What Grows in My
  Garden). Mankato, Minn.: QEB, 2013.

Internet sites

Facthound offers a safe, fun way to find Internet sites
related to this book. All of the sites on Facthound have
been researched by our staff.

Here's all you do:
Visit www.facthound.com
Type in this code: 9781484633526

Index